The Victorians

Written by
Jayne Woodhouse and Viv Wilson

Illustrated by
Tracy Fennell, Gail Newey, Susan Rowe and Sally Hynard

Edited by
Debbie Reid

Designed by
Jo Digby

Picture research by
Helen Taylor

Contents

(Answers to ☞ questions are on page 48 of this book.)

Victorian times

The Victorian period takes its name from Queen Victoria. During her very long reign, there were great changes in the lives of men, women and children.

You can see some of the most important things which happened in Victorian times at the top of page 3. As you read this book, you will find out more about them.

The timeline will help you see when some of the main events of Victorian times took place. You can add other dates to this as you read about them. It also shows that many things which we use today were invented in Victorian times.

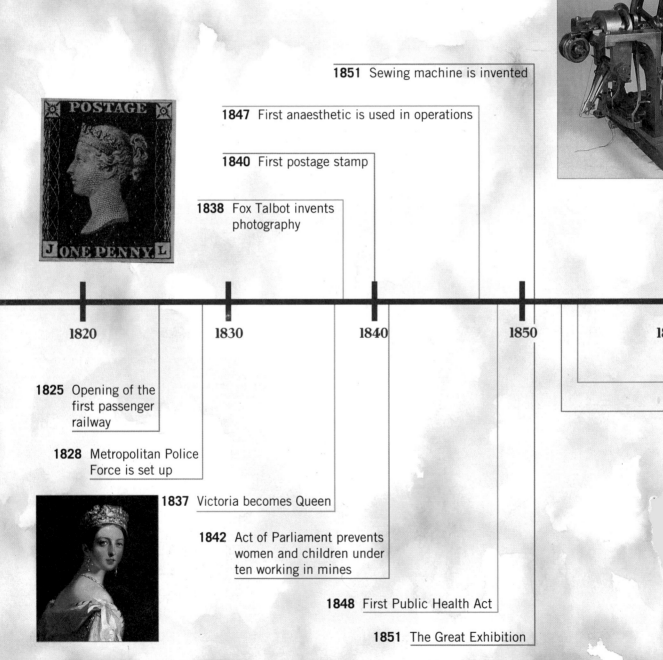

1851 Sewing machine is invented

1847 First anaesthetic is used in operations

1840 First postage stamp

1838 Fox Talbot invents photography

POSTAGE — ONE PENNY

1820   1830   1840   1850   18

1825 Opening of the first passenger railway

1828 Metropolitan Police Force is set up

1837 Victoria becomes Queen

1842 Act of Parliament prevents women and children under ten working in mines

1848 First Public Health Act

1851 The Great Exhibition

Important changes

Factories were set up to produce goods which were sold throughout the world.

New transport and communication systems were invented so that goods, people and news travelled faster.

Britain became the centre of an Empire which stretched all over the world.

People moved from the countryside into the towns to be near the new places of work. The towns grew at a great rate, and living conditions were often very poor.

Working conditions for many people were very harsh at the beginning, but improvements were made, particularly for women and children.

Daily life was very different depending on whether you were rich or poor.

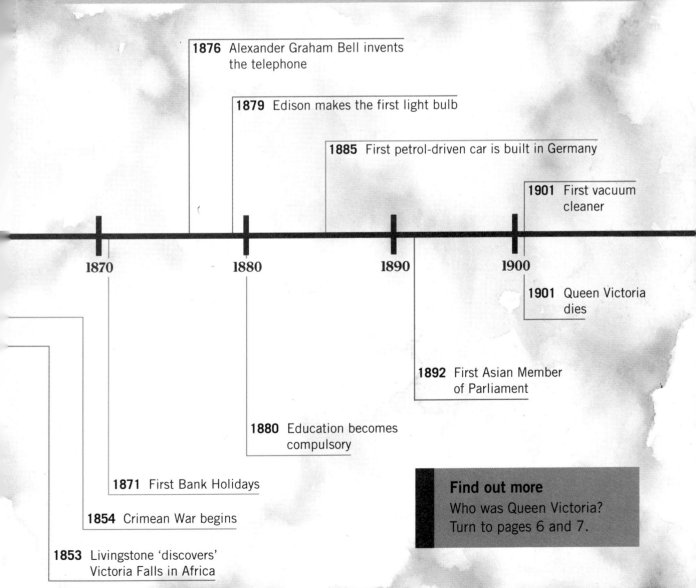

1876 Alexander Graham Bell invents the telephone

1879 Edison makes the first light bulb

1885 First petrol-driven car is built in Germany

1901 First vacuum cleaner

1870   1880   1890   1900

1901 Queen Victoria dies

1892 First Asian Member of Parliament

1880 Education becomes compulsory

1871 First Bank Holidays

1854 Crimean War begins

1853 Livingstone 'discovers' Victoria Falls in Africa

Find out more
Who was Queen Victoria?
Turn to pages 6 and 7.

Looking for evidence

In many places today, we can still find evidence of the Victorians. Street names, pub signs, buildings and monuments from the nineteenth century can tell us something about the way people lived and the important events that happened. You will find out more about the pictures on this page as you read the book.

What sort of clues from Victorian times can you find in your area?

Many schools were built in the nineteenth century. Perhaps your school is like this one.

This clock was made to celebrate Queen Victoria's Diamond Jubilee in 1897 – she had been Queen for sixty years.

MOUNT PLEASANT MIDDLE SCHOOL

KHARTOUM RD.

There was a famous battle at Khartoum in 1885. Can you work out which British soldier died in the battle? Turn to pages 8–9 for some clues.

This street lamp is also a water fountain! Although it is over a hundred years old, the colours look bright because it has been restored recently.

PRINCE CONSORT

This pub sign shows Prince Albert, Queen Victoria's husband. He was given the special title of 'Prince Consort'. You can find out more about him on pages 6-7.

Water fountains were built in the street because many people did not have fresh water in their homes. You can find out more about this on pages 24–25.

Who was Queen Victoria?

Queen Victoria reigned longer than any other British king or queen. This page tells you about some of the main events in her long life.

☞ *How long did she reign? Look at the timeline to find out.*

1861 Albert dies aged 41

1840 Marries Prince Albert

June 1837 Becomes Queen

1819 Born in Kensington Palace, London

| 1820 | 1830 | 1840 | 1850 | 1860 |

1823

1839

This portrait shows Victoria when she was four years old. The young princess was brought up very strictly. Her family knew she would be Queen one day and she was not allowed to have many friends of her own age.

Victoria became Queen when she was only eighteen. This portrait shows her as a young woman of twenty. At first Victoria was quite lonely, but then she met her German cousin, Albert, and fell in love with him.

Find out more

How did Prince Albert die? Turn to page 25.

Where else can you find a picture of Queen Victoria? Turn to page 39.

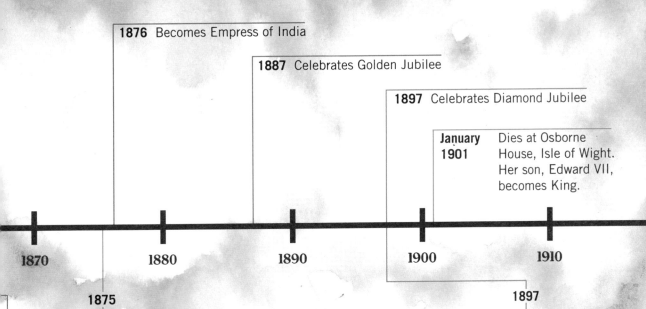

1876 Becomes Empress of India

1887 Celebrates Golden Jubilee

1897 Celebrates Diamond Jubilee

January 1901 Dies at Osborne House, Isle of Wight. Her son, Edward VII, becomes King.

1870   1880   1890   1900   1910

1875

1897

857

Prince Albert died when he was only 41. Queen Victoria was so upset that, for many years afterwards, she hardly ever appeared in public. After Albert's death, most portraits of Victoria show her dressed in black, like the one shown here.

There were great celebrations throughout the Empire on Queen Victoria's Golden and Diamond Jubilees.

☞ *Why do you think these were special occasions?*

Queen Victoria and Prince Albert had nine children – five boys and four girls.

The street

In many places you can still find houses which were built in Victorian times. Rockstone Place and Rockstone Lane are two streets which were both built at around the same time in Victorian Southampton.

Although their names are so alike, the people who lived there were very different. You can see that the large houses in Rockstone Place must have been the homes of quite wealthy people. The much smaller houses in Rockstone Lane would have been lived in by working-class people with different jobs and skills.

Rockstone Place and Rockstone Lane as they look today. There have been many changes to the houses in Rockstone Lane (left) over the last hundred years.

General Charles Gordon, a famous soldier, lived at 5 Rockstone Place with his mother and sister. He was a great hero to people in Victorian times and died in battle in 1885. You won't find his name on the census returns (see page 9) because he was away from home on the day it was taken.

You can find out much more about the people who lived in these streets by looking at the census returns. The census is like a register which covers the whole country. It takes place every ten years. The first one was taken in 1801 and the last in 1991. The evidence is kept secret for one hundred years.

☞ *Can you work out which is the latest census historians can look at?*

1871 14 Rockstone Lane – Enumerator's Returns

Name		Relation to Head of family	Age		Occupation	Place where born
Sarah	Grace	Head	Widow	38	Dressmaker	Southampton
Sarah	Grace	Daughter	Unm	20	Dressmaker	Southampton
Walker	Grace	Son	Unm	16	Clerk	Southampton
Emma	Grace	Daughter		14	Scholar	Southampton
Clara	Grace	Daughter		11	Scholar	Southampton
Frances	Street	Brother	Unm	33	Tailor	Southampton

1871 5 Rockstone Place – Enumerator's Returns

Name	Relation to Head of family		Age	Occupation	Place where born
Elizabeth Gordon	Head	Widow	78	Widow	London
Mary	Gordon	Daughter	Unm	48	Woolwich, Kent
Martha	Rumbold	Servant	Unm	39	Cook	Boscombe, Wilts
Mary	Elleston	Servant	Unm	42	Parlour Maid	Southampton
Marina	Burrows	Servant	Unm	39	Housemaid	Wimborne, Dorset

Key
Mar = Married
Unm = Unmarried

These copies of the census returns come from 1871.

The census returns shown here tell us something about the people who lived in each house and the jobs they did.

You can see that only the people in Rockstone Place had servants to look after them. Look at the jobs done by the family at 14 Rockstone Lane. Many wealthy people had their clothes made by hand. Children still at school were called scholars.

Find out more
What was it like to be a servant in Rockstone Place? Turn to pages 10 and 11.

How did the poorest people live in Victorian times? Turn to pages 26 and 27.

Servants

Many Victorian households were run by servants. Over one million people worked in domestic service at the end of the nineteenth century. One in three of these were young women or girls under twenty years of age. A wealthy household might have employed several servants, but even ordinary people such as shopkeepers, teachers and skilled workers might have had a servant too.

Some girls started work in service as young as ten. Often they worked near home and usually helped with all the household tasks. Later they might leave home to live in a larger house to take up special duties. Girls might start as scullery maids helping in the kitchen and work their way up to be housemaids or even cooks.

Servants often worked eighteen hours a day with only half a day off once a week, for very low wages. Hot water for washing and coal for the fires had to be carried up long flights of stairs, several times a day. Although this was a hard life, servants were given three meals a day and a roof over their heads. For orphans, the children of poor families and those from the workhouse, a servant's job might be a good choice.

The washroom of a large house in Ireland. Clothes were scrubbed by hand on the washboard (leaning on back wall). Then water was squeezed out of them using the mangle (left).

What special jobs did General Gordon's servants do? Look at the census return from the Gordon household on page 9.

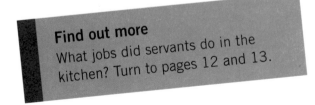

Find out more

What jobs did servants do in the kitchen? Turn to pages 12 and 13.

A servant's day

6.00 am Rise immediately and wash.

6.30 am Make up kitchen fire and wake other servants. Put washing water on fire to heat.

7.00 am Black lead fireplaces and lay fires. Polish front door step and door knocker.

8.00 am Take up hot water to bedrooms. Help cook prepare breakfast.

8.30 am Remove slops from bedrooms. Eat your own breakfast, then wash up.

9.30 am Scrub kitchen table, floor and passageways.

10.30 am Prepare vegetables for lunch. Help housemaid with heavy lifting and cleaning. Clear all bedroom fireplaces.

Fireplaces had to be cleaned and black leaded every day.

12.30 pm Eat your own lunch.

1.00 pm Wash up. Carry fresh coals to fires. Clean servants' bedrooms. Change uniform to afternoon dress and cap.

2.30 pm Either clean and polish silverware, wash downstairs windows, or do the household mending.

4.00 pm Free time and tea.

4.30 pm Help cook prepare dinner. Light gas lamps.

7.00 pm Light bedroom fires. Eat your own dinner. Wash up and scour pans.

9.00 pm Clean up kitchen, bring in fresh coals for the morning.

11.00 pm Go to bed.

Food

In wealthy Victorian homes, like the one shown in the picture, the kitchen was in the basement of the house. Here the cook worked hard all day, preparing food for everyone. Large amounts of food were eaten at breakfast, followed by a light lunch at midday. The main meal, called dinner, was served in the evening.

This is a kitchen in a wealthy Victorian home.

Pots and pans were often made of copper. They had to be polished every day by the scullery maid.

There were no refrigerators in Victorian times, so a lot of food was bought fresh each day. There was usually a cool pantry, where butter and cream were kept on a cold marble slab. Sometimes there was an ice house, where big blocks of ice were kept cold underground.

What did rich people eat . . . ?

Even ordinary meals in rich houses might have many different courses. This is what four people had for dinner on 1 April, 1885:

Tomato Soup
Fried Smelts and Drawn Butter Sauce
Mushrooms on Toast
Roast Beef, Cauliflower and Potatoes
Apple Charlotte
Toasted Cheese

Dessert:
Candied Peel, Oranges,
Peanuts,
Raisins and Ginger

. . and what did poorer people eat?

Poor families often found it hard to find enough money to feed everyone. Here is what one family in Manchester ate each week, in 1844:

'Breakfast is generally porridge, bread and milk. Dinner, on week days, potatoes and bacon, and bread. On a Sunday, a little meat. Teatime every day, tea, and bread and butter. Supper, oatmeal porridge and milk. Sunday, sometimes a little bread and cheese; never have this on week days.'

Food was cooked on a big cooker called a range. It was heated by wood or coal, and the scullery maid had to polish it every day. The range had hot plates on the top and two ovens to cook stews and bake bread, cakes and pastry.

The cook prepared all the food by hand, including bread, cakes and pastry.

Find out more

What did people have to eat in the workhouse? Turn to page 27.

How did the diet of people in the towns improve? Turn to page 40.

Clothes

By looking at the clothes people wore in the nineteenth century, we can tell a great deal about the lives they led. For example, only a wealthy Victorian family would have been able to dress like the people in the picture. They are all wearing clothes which were fashionable in the 1850s.

Men wore a frock coat with long trousers to cover their shoes. Notice the bow tie and top hat.

Ladies wore a crinoline which was very popular in the 1850s and 1860s. Underneath they wore a cage of steel or whalebone hoops which gave the wide shape to their skirts. A corset pulled in their waist to make it look small. This was only one of the many outfits they changed into each day.

There were no special clothes for children: boys and girls were dressed like miniature adults. It was not easy to run and play wearing clothes like these.

How were clothes made?

This picture shows how clothes like this were made. Everything was sewn by hand. Dressmakers worked for long hours in small, airless rooms. If they were lucky, they might earn 7 shillings (35p) a week.

☞ *Can you find the clue in the picture which tells you how late these women have to work?*

The greatest change to how clothes were made came with the invention of the sewing machine in 1851. However, it did not become popular in Britain for another twenty years.

'In the busy time I worked to twelve at night, and then had to get up again at four the next morning and work again till twelve. We only had ten minutes for any meal – even dinner. My health suffered very much.'

A dressmaker's story

Changing fashions

There were many changes in fashion during Victorian times, particularly for women. By the end of the century sporting activities, especially cycling, helped to create clothes in which women could lead more active lives.

A woman in cycling clothes in 1890

Find out more

How did wealthy Victorians dress when they visited the seaside? Turn to pages 42 and 43.

How did other people dress in Victorian times? There are many pictures in other pages of this book which will help you find out.

Children at work – in industry

Although machines had been invented before Victorian times, it was during the first half of Queen Victoria's reign that more and more factories were built in the towns. People started to move from the countryside and took jobs in the new factories. Towns started to grow bigger.

Children worked in factories as well as grown ups. In the beginning of Victorian times, children were treated very harshly by some employers.

Dangerous work

Children as young as four years old used to do jobs like the one in the picture because they were so small they could get underneath the machines.

Can you see the little child crawling under the working machinery in the cotton mill? He is cleaning up all the bits of cotton so they won't jam the machine.

As they grew older, children did many different jobs in factories which were often dangerous and very hard work. They were beaten if they did not work hard enough, or if they fell asleep during their long working day. Sometimes accidents happened to children when they fell asleep working at their machines.

Children also worked underground in coal mines. At the beginning of Victorian times, they started working underground at the age of five or six. Little children sat in the dark all day, opening the doors in the tunnels to let the coal carts go through.

These pictures show the sorts of jobs that boys and girls did in the coal mines. Sometimes it took two men to lift the baskets on to the girls' backs.

'They are chained, belted and harnessed like dogs in a go-cart, black, saturated with wet and more than half-naked, crawling upon their hands and feet, and dragging their loads behind them.'

A report describing children working in the mines (1842)

Lord Shaftesbury worked very hard to improve the lives of working children. In 1842, he helped to pass a law to stop children under ten working in coal mines. But children older than ten could still work for up to twelve hours each day. It took many more years to change the way people thought about working children.

Find out more

What other jobs did children do in town and country? Turn to pages 18 and 20.

What else did Lord Shaftesbury do to help poor children? Turn to page 18.

What was the biggest change in children's lives in Victorian times? Turn to page 22.

Children at work – in towns

Many poor children and orphans went out to work in the towns from a very young age. This page shows some of the jobs they did. Some boys worked as sweeps and were sent to climb up the soot-filled chimneys to clean them out. Many children worked in small workshops and yards, making things like bricks and nails.

Since these children did not work in big factories or mines, the laws which Parliament passed about working conditions did not apply to most of them until 1870. Eventually, Parliament passed a law forbidding chimney sweeps to send young boys up chimneys.

People like Lord Shaftesbury tried to help these working children in the towns by setting up schools called Ragged Schools where they could learn to read and write in the evenings and at weekends.

'In wide flues you climb with your elbows and your legs spread out . . . but in narrow ones, you must have your sides in the angles . . . I niver got stuck myself, but a many of them did; yes, and were tak'n out dead.'

A child chimney sweep

'Another girl brought the clay to the bench. She was about thirteen. She lifted a lump of cold clay, weighing about 25 pounds, and balanced it upon her head. Then she lifted a lump of equal weight . . . and, with the two burdens, walked and put them on the moulding bench.'

A brickyard child

'I buy my flowers at Covent Garden . . . I pay one shilling (5p) for a dozen bunches, whatever flowers are in. Out of every two bunches I can make three, at one penny a piece . . . .'

An orphan flower girl

Children at work – countryside

In Victorian times, many people still lived in the country, although the towns and cities were growing. Thousands of children worked for farmers in the countryside. The few pennies they brought home every week were needed to buy food for their families and to pay the rent.

Both boys and girls started work when they were as young as six years old. Often they would work from very early in the morning until it grew dark, with only a short break for food. Then they might have to walk five or six miles to get home.

Spring
Weeding and bird scaring

Children did many different jobs on the land. In the spring, they weeded the fields and used wooden rattles to scare birds away from the newly sown seeds. In summer, they helped with the harvest, tying up the bundles (sheaves) of corn and picking up the stalks of corn which had been dropped (gleaning). The pictures show you some of the things they did each season. Farmers didn't have machines to do jobs like these.

The jobs were very boring and often hard to do. Children working on the land had to stay outside in all kinds of weather and they were not allowed to stop work if it rained. If they did, they would lose their wages.

Summer
*Helping with
the harvest*

Here is Albert Merritt's story of his work on a farm in 1867, when he was ten years old. Albert was a ploughboy.

'I leave home at 5 am, go to the farm and help clean out my stable and get the horses ready. Then I go with the horses on the land, and work till noon. I get a quarter of an hour for dinner, bread and cheese and cider. I keep on ploughing till three, then take the horses home and feed them. I do not get home till 7 o'clock. I have my supper of bacon and potatoes and go to bed at 8 o'clock.'

Autumn
*Picking potatoes and looking
after pigs in the fields*

Find out more

What jobs did children in the towns do? Turn to pages 16 and 18.

What was the most important change for children in Victorian times? Turn to page 22.

Winter
*Picking stones from the fields to stop
the farmer's plough being damaged*

Children at school

During the nineteenth century, more and more children began to go to school. At first, many only attended for a year or two because they had to work. From 1870 onwards, many more schools were built. In 1880, a law was passed saying that all children had to go to school until they were ten. Some parents were unhappy because the family lost the children's wages. At first, they also had to pay a few pennies each week towards the cost of education.

Look carefully at the photograph of the classroom above. Notice the clothes the teachers and children are wearing. What other differences can you find between this classroom and your own?

Writing

Children first learned to write and do arithmetic using a slate pencil on a slate which could be wiped clean. Later they practised using a pen and ink in a copy book.

Learning

Many things, such as poems and lists of dates in history, had to be learned by heart. Girls did needlework while boys were taught woodwork or gardening. They were tested on their lessons once a year by school inspectors. If they had not learned their lessons well enough, they could not go up into the next class.

NAME	OFFENCE	PUNISHMENT
Fred Egerton	Spitting on another boy	2 on Buttox & 2 on hand
Raymond Morris	Repeated Disobedience	2 on hand & 2 on Buttox
William Rockley	Inattention	2 on hand
Frank Biddlecombe	Disobedience	2 on hand
Alan Jones	Sulking	2 on hand
Maurice Jones	Eating Sweets in School	2 on hand
Reginald Holloway	Talking	2 on hand
Albert Hatch	Mocking J Blake	2 on each hand
Ernest Jones	Disobedience	2 on each hand
James Dibdin	Very Dirty Book	2 on hand
Maurice Jones	Very Bad Work	2 on hand

This Punishment Book shows you what happened to some Victorian schoolboys.

Punishment

Classes were very large and teachers were often very strict. Children were sometimes caned for bad behaviour.

☞ *Which child is caned twice?*

Look closely at the Punishment Book above to find out.

Find out more
What did some children do when they were not at school? Turn to page 42.

Public health

During Victorian times, more and more people moved into the towns to work in factories. The towns very soon became overcrowded. Many houses were built, but they were often too close together, so there was not enough fresh air and light. In the poorest areas, whole families sometimes lived in one room.

A Glasgow slum in the 1860s

Houses like the ones in the picture were lived in by very poor people. They were built without any proper lavatories. All sorts of filth and rubbish lay rotting in the streets. The smell was dreadful. There was not even any fresh, clean water to drink or to wash in.

'The walls (of the houses) are crumbling, doorposts and window-frames loose and broken ... Heaps of garbage and ashes lie in all directions, and the foul liquids emptied before the doors gather in stinking pools ....'

How one visitor described London in the 1840s

People queuing for water at the pump

This picture shows how people had to carry their water home from the pump. Very often the water was brown and dirty, and in summer the pump ran dry.

In streets like these, diseases such as cholera spread very rapidly. Cholera causes sickness and diarrhoea which makes people so weak that they can die. In 1832, cholera killed 32 000 people. In 1848, when there were even more people living in the towns, it killed 62 000. Most of these were poor people, but no one was safe: in 1861, Prince Albert died of typhoid fever caused by the bad drains at Windsor Castle.

Slowly, during the nineteenth century, laws were passed which brought about some improvements. Sewers were built, clean water was piped to many houses and the streets were cleaned. But these changes took a long time. In some towns, the old houses were finally pulled down at the end of the century and better homes were built.

At first, no one knew what caused cholera. Some doctors thought it was the result of poisonous gases in the air. In 1854, Dr John Snow made the important discovery that cholera was caused by infected water. Because early Victorian towns had no proper sewers or water supply, germs spread from the drains into the drinking water.

☞ *Why do you think most people who died of cholera were poor?*

Find out more
Was life like this in all parts of Victorian towns? Turn to page 8.

Where else did poor people live? Turn to page 26.

The workhouse

In Victorian times, there were no old age pensions and there was no sick pay or dole money. If you had no money to look after yourself – perhaps because you were old, ill or unemployed – you had to go to the workhouse. Life in a workhouse was made hard on purpose, so that paupers (as poor people were called) would only go there as a last resort.

The workhouse at Andover in Hampshire looked like a prison, with its high walls and small windows.

The workhouse timetable
Summer

6.00 am	Rise
6.30 – 7.00 am	Breakfast
Work	
12.00 am – 1.00 pm	Dinner
Work	
6.00 pm – 7.00 pm	Supper
8.00 pm	Bed

In winter, times of rising and starting work were one hour later.

Men, women, boys and girls all lived in different parts of the workhouse, so families were separated. They all had to wear a uniform and children's hair was cut short. Once they were inside, they had to work every day except Sunday, doing jobs that were both hard and boring. At Andover, women washed clothes in the laundry. The men crushed old animal bones to make fertilizer to put on the fields.

☞ *Can you work out from the timetable how many hours people had to work in summer and in winter?*

Meals

In return for working hard, the people in the workhouse were given food. As you can see from the diet sheet below, meals were mostly bread, cheese and gruel (oatmeal boiled in water) day after day. They must have looked forward to every Tuesday and Saturday, when they were given a small amount of meat. There was never enough to eat. At Andover, the men were so hungry that they ate the rotting meat from the bones they were crushing.

		Breakfast		Dinner						Supper	
		Bread	Gruel	Bread	Cheese	Cooked meat	Veg	Soup	Bacon	Bread	Cheese
		ozs	pts	ozs	ozs	ozs	ozs	pts	ozs	ozs	ozs
SUN	Men	6	1½	7	2					6	1½
	Women	5	1½	6	1½					5	1½
MON	Men	6	1½	7	2					6	1½
	Women	5	1½	6	1½					5	1½
TUE	Men	6	1½			8	½			6	1½
	Women	5	1½			6	½			5	1½
WED	Men	6	1½	7	2					6	1½
	Women	5	1½	6	1½					5	1½
THU	Men	6	1½					1½		6	1½
	Women	5	1½					1½		5	1½
FRI	Men	6	1½	7	2					6	1½
	Women	5	1½	6	1½					5	1½
SAT	Men	6	1½				½		5	6	1½
	Women	5	1½				½		4	5	1½

A workhouse diet sheet

A workhouse dining room in St Pancras, 1895. Meals were eaten in silence.

Find out more
While paupers were eating gruel, what did some other people in Victorian times have to eat? Turn to pages 12 and 13.

Religion

In Victorian times, a lot more people went to church every Sunday than they do today. Christianity was the main religion, but there were several different types of worship and belief. The Church of England was the official church of the country and the one which Queen Victoria belonged to.

In the new industrial towns like Manchester and Birmingham, many people went to services in churches or chapels run by Methodists and Baptists. These services were more popular with people who wanted a simpler form of worship. Some people attended the Catholic church, while others followed their own religion, like Jews who had come from Europe to settle in Britain.

The Victorians built many churches. They liked to copy buildings from the Middle Ages, with their high, pointed arches – there may be one near where you live.

Churches raised money to help the poor and build schools long before the government did these things. Some churches, however, also taught people that God had chosen whether they should be rich or poor. A verse from 'All Things Bright and Beautiful', a popular Victorian hymn, explains this idea:

'The rich man in his castle,
The poor man at his gate,
God made them high or lowly,
And ordered their estate.'

Inside a Victorian church

Sundays

In some better-off families, Sunday was a special day set aside for rest and going to church. The day often started and ended with family prayers. Children were not allowed to play, but were expected to sit quietly and read from the Bible.

At the beginning of Victoria's reign, Sundays were the only chance for some of the poorest children to get any education at all. Sunday Schools at church taught them to read and write.

So, churches were not just places where services were held – they also played an important part in many people's lives.

Churches also organised treats, such as this picnic in the country.

Find out more
What part did the Church play in the British Empire? Turn to page 30.

Trade and Empire

As Britain became a more industrial country, factory owners needed new places to sell the goods that were being made. The Victorians looked for other countries to trade with, like India and Africa. During the first part of Queen Victoria's reign, Britain took control of many areas of the world. This was to stop other countries trading there and to make land available for the British to go and live. These areas together became known as the British Empire.

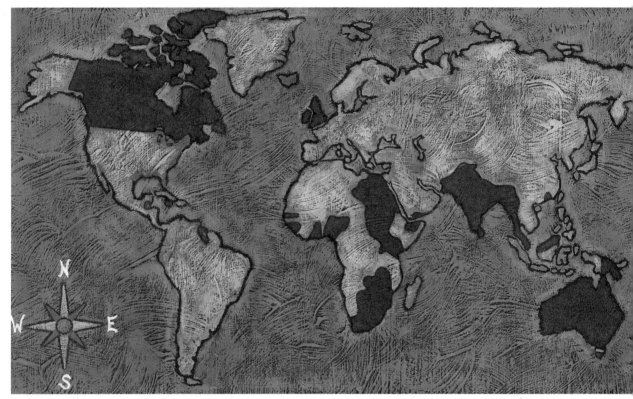

Countries of the British Empire in 1901

Many people left their homes to live in countries of the Empire. Missionaries from British churches were also sent because Victorians believed that the native people should become Christians. Not all missionaries respected the different ways of life they found when they arrived.

On board an emigrant ship, 1871

India

Up until 1850, many different regions of India were ruled by their own princes. Trade between Britain and India was controlled by a British Governor General. Goods such as cotton and tea were sent to Britain from India, and articles made in British factories were sent back in return. Traders became very rich and powerful.

Queen Victoria is declared Empress of India.

The Indian Mutiny

Lord Dalhousie, who became Governor General in 1847, wanted to change local Indian customs and religious beliefs, and to take control of parts of the country. Indian people did not want this to happen and, in 1857, some Indian Army soldiers rebelled against harsh treatment by the British. This was called the Indian Mutiny and, because wives and children of some British officers were killed, people back in Britain became very concerned. The Mutiny was stopped, but after this the British Government took control of all of India, and Queen Victoria became its ruler.

In 1876, Queen Victoria became Empress of India. India was known as the 'Jewel in the Crown' because the Victorians thought it was the most important country in the Empire.

Find out more
Where did ordinary Victorian people go to find out more about India and Africa? Turn to page 44.

Trade and Empire – Africa

Africa was not fully explored by Europeans until Victorian times. The first trading ports had been built on the west coast and supplied ivory and gold to Europe. Slaves had also been shipped out from these ports to work on plantations in America and the West Indies. Although the British Parliament banned the slave trade in 1807, slaves were not made free in countries controlled by Britain until 1833, four years before Victoria became Queen.

Britain did not rule over the whole of Africa, as it did India. Other European countries also had territories under their control. There were French, German, Belgian and Portuguese colonies as well as British ones. The African people fought back against European rule in many places, and soldiers were often sent to fight wars to protect the British colonies. In 1881–98, there were battles in the Sudan, and General Gordon was killed at the siege of the city of Khartoum. There were also fierce battles with the Zulu people just after the end of Queen Victoria's reign.

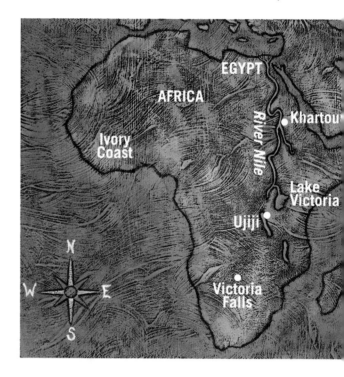

David Livingstone, a missionary and explorer, crossed Africa from the west side to the east. He was the first European to see the famous waterfalls which he re-named the Victoria Falls. For several years, no one in England knew whether he was alive or dead. In 1869, Sir Henry Morton Stanley was told to 'find Livingstone'. The two men finally met, two years later, in Central Africa at a place called Ujiji.

Famous explorers

There were many famous explorers who set out to find out more about Africa. In 1856, John Speke and Richard Burton set out to find out where the River Nile began. John Speke later found Lake Nyanza, which he believed to be the source. He re-named the lake, Lake Victoria.

John Speke at Lake Victoria

Find out more

Find out about General Gordon's home in Southampton on page 8.

How did people from Africa and India come to live in Britain? Turn to pages 36 and 37.

The Crimean War

In 1854–56, the British were at war with the Russian army in part of the Turkish Empire called the Crimea. The Russians were finally defeated, but 25 000 soldiers died and many more were wounded. Wounded soldiers were taken to a hospital in a town called Scutari. Conditions there were terrible, with no proper beds or food. More soldiers died of diseases like cholera than they did from their wounds.

Florence Nightingale

Florence Nightingale had a long battle with her family to be allowed to be a nurse. In Victorian times, nursing was a very rough job. Unlike Florence Nightingale, most nurses did not come from good family backgrounds. They did not know much about medicine or hygiene and were sometimes drunk or fell asleep when they were meant to be looking after sick people.

After Florence was finally allowed to take up nursing, she led a group of other nurses to help the soldiers in the Crimea. She cleaned up the hospital at Scutari, with the help of her nurses, and provided proper food and clean bedding. Each night, Florence Nightingale would visit the wards carrying her lamp to see that the soldiers were comfortable. Because of this, she became known as 'The Lady with the Lamp'. As a result of the improvements Florence made in the hospital, far fewer soldiers died.

She returned to England as a famous person and set up a training hospital for nurses. Florence's work helped nursing become a respectable job for women.

*Florence Nightingale –
The Lady with the Lamp*

Mary Seacole

Today, many people have heard of Florence Nightingale but Mary Seacole's story is not so well known.

Mary also nursed soldiers in the Crimean War. When Mary heard about the fighting in the Crimea, she decided she had to go there. No one seemed to want her help so she paid her own fare. When Mary arrived, she set up a kitchen to cook hot food for the troops. She even walked on to the battlefield to nurse the wounded soldiers while the guns were firing.

After the war, Mary came back to England with no money and no home. Grateful soldiers raised money to help her and she was given medals for her bravery. Sadly, she died alone and unknown.

Mary Seacole was born in Jamaica and grew up helping her mother look after sick people.

Find out more

Who discovered how cholera spread? Turn to page 25.

Mary Seacole came from the West Indies. What else can you find out about black people in Victorian Britain? Turn to pages 36 and 37.

Black settlers

During the nineteenth century, developments in trade and transport brought people to this country from many parts of the world. People came from Ireland, from China and from Europe to settle in Britain and begin new lives. The growth of the British Empire also brought settlers from the countries under British rule. Some of these people were from Africa and Asia.

. . from Africa

Part of Britain's wealth at the start of the Victorian period came from the slave trade. This also brought a number of black people to Britain, where many of them worked as servants. Although all slaves in the British Empire were made free in 1833, slavery continued for another thirty years in America. During that time, runaway slaves from America also found their way to this country.

From 1875 onwards, the British took over more and more of Africa. This meant that many more black settlers and visitors came to Britain. By far the largest group were black sailors who sometimes stayed in the ports to live and marry. In this way, the first black communities grew up around places such as Cardiff and Liverpool. These people were poor and were sometimes unemployed for long periods. They were often victims of racial prejudice too.

. . from Asia

Seamen also came to England from Asia. They received very little pay and lived in terrible conditions. In London, as many as eight Indian seamen lived in one single room. They slept on a wooden floor with only one blanket to cover them in winter.

A small group of Indians living in England worked to free India from British rule. Amongst these was Dadabhai Naoroji who, in 1892, became the first Asian Member of Parliament. He worked hard all his life to tell people in England about the wrongs that were being carried out in India.

William Cuffay's father was a slave in the West Indies. William was born on a ship travelling to England. He fought hard for the rights of ordinary working people. However, he was arrested for his beliefs and transported to Tasmania for life. He died there in 1870, a well-respected member of the community.

Public services

In early Victorian times, each town and local district took care of whatever public services it had. These services were not the same all over Britain – it depended on what local people were willing to pay for.

By the end of the Victorian period, however, many public services could be found everywhere as people realised that they made life easier.

Police

When Queen Victoria came to the throne, there were hardly any policemen in the country. Sir Robert Peel had set up a special police force in London, in 1829, to try to make the city a safer place. His men had to walk their 'beat' for nine hours a day, without stopping. At first these 'Peelers' were unpopular, but slowly people realised that the streets had become safer places thanks to the new policemen.

Sir Robert Peel wanted his policemen to wear a uniform that looked more like ordinary clothes and not like a soldier's uniform. The policeman only had a wooden truncheon to defend himself and a rattle to call for help, as shown in this picture. At night, he carried a lantern called a 'bull's eye'.

Soon other cities in Britain realised how useful the Metropolitan Police Force was in London, and set up forces of their own. By 1856, most places in Britain had to have their own police force, by law.

A Victorian 'Peeler'

The Penny Black

Post

If people wanted to send a letter before 1840, the person the letter was sent to had to pay for it. This might cost as much as one shilling (5p), which was very expensive. If people could not pay, the letter was taken away again!

A man called Rowland Hill suggested that instead of paying to receive a letter, people should pay before they sent one. This way, their letter was sure to arrive safely. To show that the postage had been paid, a stamp would be stuck on the letter. Every stamp would cost one old penny.

This is a picture of the very first stamp which could be bought and stuck on a letter. It was called the Penny Black because of its colour and its cost. Nowadays, real copies of this stamp are very rare and are worth thousands of pounds.

Soon, many more people were writing letters and using the 'Penny Post', and more and more Post Offices were opened. At first, people had to visit the Post Office to collect their letters or pay a deliverer to bring them. In 1897, letter delivery became free as part of the celebrations of Queen Victoria's Diamond Jubilee.

Pillar boxes

Pillar boxes were first seen in London in 1855. They were put up to save people having to walk to the Post Office to post their letters. This box can still be seen in Cheltenham today.

☞ *Can you identify the initials on the front of the box? Whose initials do you think they are?*

A surviving Victorian pillar box

Find out more
How did letters travel quickly around the country? Turn to page 40.

The railway age

One of the biggest changes to take place in Victorian times was the development of the railways. In 1754, it took four and a half days to travel from London to Manchester by horse-drawn coach. A hundred years later, the same journey took twelve hours thanks to the invention of the steam engine.

The railways grew at an astonishing speed, especially in the 1840s when most of the lines we still use today were laid. By 1848, there were 8045 kilometres of track in use.

The spread of the railways meant that goods could be carried quickly from place to place. Factories could now make more products and sell them more cheaply. Fresh food became more easily available as milk, vegetables and fish were carried to the towns. New ideas also travelled rapidly around Britain as the railways brought books, newspapers and letters to every town.

☞ *People today still travel in* carriages or coaches *when they go by train. Can you work out from the picture where these names come from?*

Find out more

Where did many people go by train in their leisure time? Turn to page 42.

Isambard Kingdom Brunel was one of the greatest engineers of the railway age. His designs can still be seen today in some of the bridges he built.

Third Class travel

In 1844, an Act of Parliament introduced cheap Third Class travel. This was the first time that ordinary people could afford to move around the country easily.

Third Class passengers sat on wooden benches and there was little protection from the weather. First and Second Class passengers travelled in greater comfort, but there was still no heating. In the winter, people kept warm with hot water bottles.

'Such trains shall travel at an average speed of not less than twelve miles an hour for the whole distance . . . The carriages shall have seats and shall be protected from the weather. The fare shall not exceed one penny for each mile travelled.'

Some of the rules which railways had to follow for Third Class travel

The seaside

At first, ordinary people had very little spare time and no chance to travel except perhaps to look for work. The first real holidays began in 1871, when Bank Holidays gave workers a few days off each year.

The other important change at this time was the spread of railways across the country, from towns to the coast. As travelling by train became cheaper, working-class people could afford to buy tickets. More and more families began to go on day trips to the seaside. Places such as Ramsgate, Margate, Blackpool and Bournemouth grew quickly from little fishing ports into big resorts as the number of holiday makers increased.

This is part of a painting called 'Ramsgate Sands' by William Powell Frith which shows Victorian families at the seaside.

This painting was made in 1854 and shows Victorian families on the beach at Ramsgate. You can see that, at this time, people did not wear different clothes on holiday.

If you look closely at the picture, you can see the Punch and Judy show in the background. How does this picture compare with photographs of seaside holidays today?

Bathing

The Victorians thought it was important for women to keep their bodies covered up. They wore special bathing costumes like the ones in the picture which must have felt very heavy and uncomfortable when they got wet. Men and women bathed in different parts of the beach. They went out into the sea in bathing machines which were like huts on wheels, so that no one would see them get undressed and go into the water.

Victorian women in bathing costumes

Find out more

Could all Victorian children afford a day at the seaside? Turn to page 26.

Find out more about Victorian clothes. Turn to pages 14 and 15.

Thomas Cook was the first person to develop holiday trips using the railways. In 1851, the trains he organised brought hundreds of people to see the Great Exhibition (see page 44). His first grand tour of Europe took place in 1856, and from then on his holidays spread all over the world. People today can still book their holidays through the company that bears his name.

The Great Exhibition

The Great Exhibition was Prince Albert's idea. It was a way of showing everyone how successful British industry and trade were by putting on show all the things that could be made in this country.

In 1851, a new building made of iron and glass was erected in Hyde Park, London for the exhibition. It soon became known as the Crystal Palace. Inside were exhibits from all over the world which people flocked to see. On some days, tickets only cost one shilling (5p), which even working-class people could afford to buy. For many of them, it was their first trip to London.

Who designed the Crystal Palace?

Joseph Paxton began life as a gardener. He won the competition to design the building for the Great Exhibition. He designed it around three large elm trees which the Victorians wanted to conserve.

Was the Exhibition a good idea?

Queen Victoria visited the Exhibition several times and liked it very much. But not everyone thought the Great Exhibition was a good idea. Some people thought it was wrong to erect such a huge building in a public park. They were afraid it would attract thieves and beggars.

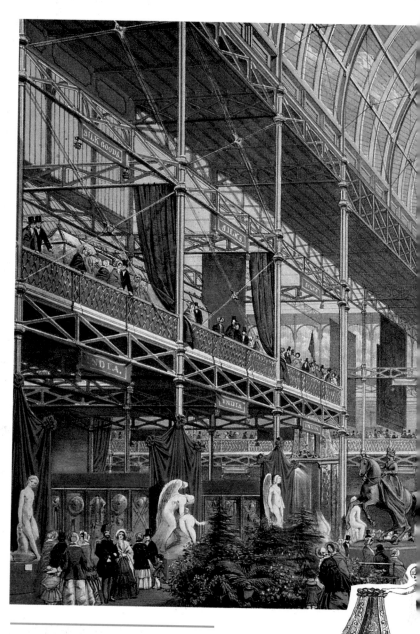

'A piece of low, dirty cunning . . . a humbug from beginning to end.'

Member of Parliament

Facts and figures

The Crystal Palace was 563 m long, 124 m wide and 19 m high (33 m at its highest). It covered an area of ground about the size of six football pitches.

It was built by over 2000 workmen, using 4428 tonnes of iron, 38 kilometres of guttering and 300 000 panes of glass.

More than six million visitors came to look at 100 000 exhibits in the five months it was open.

They drank one million bottles of soft drink and ate two million buns.

The Crystal Palace was taken down in the summer of 1852 and rebuilt at Sydenham. It was destroyed by fire in 1936.

'The view from near the end, close to the last entrance, one can never carry in one's mind – each time one is amazed afresh at the immense length and height and the fairy-like effect of the different objects that fill it.'

An extract from Queen Victoria's diary

An ornamental bird cage exhibit

The inside of the Crystal Palace during the Great Exhibition

Find out more

Who helped organise trips to the Great Exhibition? Turn to page 43.

Did British industry make life better for everyone? Turn to pages 16 and 17.

A child's cot exhibit

A Victorian Christmas

Many of the Christmas customs we have today first began in Victorian times. Look carefully at this picture of a family sitting down to their Christmas dinner in the 1860s. You will recognise lots of the things you might find in homes now on Christmas Day.

Of course, not all Victorian families could afford to celebrate Christmas like this. For poor people, Christmas was much the same as any other day, with no presents and no money to buy a special dinner.

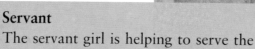

Servant
The servant girl is helping to serve the dinner. There was no holiday for her on Christmas Day.

Roast goose
For their special Christmas dinner, the family had roast goose, followed by plum pudding. People who were not so well off saved a small amount of money each week in the 'Goose Club' so that they could afford to buy a goose for Christmas Day. By the 1880s, turkey had mostly replaced goose as the traditional Christmas fare.

Crackers
After dinner the family pulled their crackers. These were invented by Thomas Smith in 1846 and contained a mixture of sweets, paper hats, mottoes and gifts.

Christmas cards

The first Christmas cards were made in 1843 for Sir Henry Cole to send to his friends. They soon became very popular. The introduction of the Penny Post meant that people could send cards all over the country. In Victorian times, the postman even delivered on Christmas day!

Christmas tree

Christmas trees first became popular in the 1840s when Prince Albert introduced them from his own country, Germany. They might be decorated with candles, fruit, nuts, sweets and presents. Holly, ivy and mistletoe were used to decorate the rest of the room.

Presents

The children have opened the stockings they hung up on Christmas Eve. Father Christmas has brought them a doll, a toy soldier, books and a ball. Poorer children would have had far fewer things than these. They might find an orange, a penny, a few sweets, or perhaps a home-made toy in their stockings.

Find out more

How were Christmas cards sent? Find out about the Penny Post on page 39.

What things did servants do for the rest of the year? Turn to pages 10 and 11.

Answers to ⌐

Page 6–7: Queen Victoria reigned for 63 and a half years, from June 1837 to January 1901.
These were special occasions because Victoria had reigned for fifty years (Golden Jubilee) and sixty years (Diamond Jubilee).
Page 9: The latest census historians can look at is 1891.
Page 10: In General Gordon's house there was a cook (Martha Rumbold), a parlour maid (Mary Elleston) and a house maid (Marina Burrows).
Page 15: The clue which tells you how late the dressmakers are working is the clock on the wall which says five minutes past twelve (midnight).
Page 23: Maurice Jones is caned twice – once for eating sweets in

school, and once for very bad work.
Page 25: Mostly poor people died of cholera because they lived in the worst parts of the towns where there was overcrowding, very little clean drinking water and poor drains.
Page 26: The people of Andover workhouse had to work 10 hours a day (60 hours each week) in the summer, and 9 hours a day (54 hours each week) in the winter.
Page 39: The initials on the pillar box are V.R. They stand for Victoria Regina, which means Queen Victoria.
Page 41: The first railway carriages were built to look like stage coaches which were the main form of passenger transport before the railway age.

Published by BBC Educational Publishing, a division of BBC Education, Woodlands, 80 Wood Lane, London W12 0TT
First published 1994
©Jayne Woodhouse and Viv Wilson/BBC Education 1994
The moral rights of the authors have been asserted.

Paperback ISBN: 0 563 35428 3
Hardback ISBN: 0 563 35445 3

Colour reproduction by Goodfellow & Egan, Cambridge
Cover origination in England by Goodfellow & Egan, Cambridge
Printed and bound by BPC Paulton Books Ltd

Photo credits
Arcaid/M Fiennes **pp. 28/29**; Hilary Bowen **pp. 4/5**, **8 (top and middle)**; The British Library Newspaper Library **p. 37 (bottom)**; The Thomas Cook Travel Archive **p. 43 (insert)**; Crown Copyright, reproduced with the permission of the Controller of Her Majesty's Stationery Office **p. 9** *2 CPY 4(8)*; By permission of the Governors of Dulwich Picture Gallery **p. 6 (left)**; Edifice **pp. 4 (left)**, **39 (bottom)**; Mary Evans Picture Library

pp. 11, 15 (top), 17 (left), 27, 32, 40/41; Stanley Gibbons Auctions **pp. 2 (top left)**, **39 (top)**; Greater London Council **p. 22**; Michael Holford **p. 2 (top right)**; Hulton Deutsch Collection **pp. 7 (bottom and right)**, **15 (bottom)**, **16, 24, 34, 37 (top)**, **44 (bottom)**, **44/45**; The Illustrated London News Picture Library **p. 31 (top)**; The Billie Love Historical Collection **p. 29**; Mansell Collection **p. 31 (bottom)**; Museum of London **pp. 22/23**; Courtesy of the National Library of Jamaica **p. 35**; By courtesy of the National Portrait Gallery, London **pp. 7 (left)**, **8 (bottom)**, **17 (right)**, **40 (bottom)**; The National Trust Photographic Library **p. 10**; Papilio/Robert Pickett **p. 43**; The Royal Collection © 1994 Her Majesty The Queen **pp. 6 (left)** *Queen Victoria 1839* by Landseer, **38** *Ramsgate Sands* by Frith; Victoria and Albert Museum **p. 45 (right)**; The Wallace Collection **p. 2 (bottom left)** *Queen Victoria in Robes of State* by Sully; The Wellcome Trust **p. 25**.
Front cover: Hulton Deutsch Collection: *A Family Portrait, 1880s* **(left)**; Barnardo's Photographic Archive: *Early Admission Child* **(right)**.

Illustrations © Tracy Fennell, 1994 (pages 2/3, 6/7, 10/11, 12, 20/21, 26, 33 and 36/37); © Gail Newey, 1994 (pages 18/19, 26, 30, 32, 35 and 38); © Susan Rowe, 1994 (pages 14, 43 and 46/47); © Sally Hynard, 1994 (pages 12/13).